D1 BOUND: THE ULTIMATE GUIDE TO COLLEGE FOOTBALL RECRUITING

2024 EDITION

BY COACH MASON FARQUHAR

D1 BOUND

Chase after your dreams.

My dream was to go D1... the highest level of college football there is. I dreamed of it, I believed in myself, but deep down I had doubt. I never really saw myself as "D1 Bound." I never fully believed in myself to get to that level.

D1 Bound is about believing in yourself. It is about testing the boundaries and chasing after the impossible. I'm not just talking to athletes here; I'm talking to any person who lacks confidence to chase their dreams.

Being D1 Bound means that you're defining your dreams as reality. This will happen. You will make this happen. You will maximize every opportunity and give yourself the best chance to become the best version of yourself.

Remember, it's about the journey. The road to success is about chasing perfection. But perfection doesn't exist, so the journey is the prize.

Push and keep on pushing. And above all, believe in yourself and who you are.

Leave no doubt!

Introduction

Welcome!
How My Story Inspires Me to Inform You

Part 1: Understanding Yourself

Close the Gap!
It's a Game of Numbers
Handle Your Business
Now, Separate from the Pack.

Part 2: Understanding the Process

Become Reachable
Recruiting Periods
Summer Camps
WHO You Know Matters
Film
A Coach's Process
Communication
What's an Offer?
Important Dates: A Recruiting Calendar

Part 3: Understanding College Football Programs

A College Football Staff
New Age College Football
Transfer Portal
Name Image Likeness (NIL)

Part 4: Understanding the GAME

Perfect Your Craft
The Relentless Pursuit

Conclusion

Thank You!

1

Introduction

Welcome to my film room! The fact you opened this book shows that you have the will to learn. It proves you care. You will learn the ins and outs of college football recruiting from a man on the inside. Open your notebooks and take some notes. Just reading isn't enough. You must apply the knowledge.

I know this is targeting athletes who are chasing their dreams, but if you end up jumping into the experience, I believe you will learn something about chasing your dreams and maximizing opportunity in your field of work.

An old quote by Benjamin Franklin stands out to me.

"Many men die at age 25 but aren't buried until they're 75." – Benjamin Franklin

Chase your dreams! You only have one life to live, and this is your opportunity to make it the life you want. If you fail at one, stand up, brush the dirt off your jersey, and try again.

I'm excited to have you learn from my experiences, mistakes, failures, and success.

My name is Coach Mace and I'm a Football Coach at a D1 school. When I was 18, I watched my dreams wither away as no Division 1 offers came through. I had the opportunity to play Division 2 Football, coach high school football, coach at a Power 5 program, and coach at a G5 Division 1 program. I've gained insight from all levels of the business. This course information is everything I wish I would have known while playing high school football that would have elevated my chances of going Division 1. Learn from my experience... give yourself the best chance to chase your dream.

Please give me some feedback as you go about this book. I would love to hear how I can make it better. Ask questions! I want to make this the best possible source of information for a topic that is not touched for athletes.

It's a changing game. I'm living in the middle of it all. I will continue to make updates to this book as we move along. Updates will take place with new editions and updates will be sent to those who sign up for them.

I want to make this SIMPLE. It's a complex business, but my job as a coach is to uncomplicate the complex. You'll notice that I start a lot of chapters by mentioning how complex the topic is, so I will try my best to make it as simple, yet useful as possible.

It's important I put this at the beginning, but anything that your Head Coach says should trump this information. He knows you best and he will be your biggest advocate when getting you college opportunities. He is way more important than you realize. Trust him!

If you don't understand something... ASK!

Comment on the chapters if you have questions or email me at <u>macefarq@gmail.com</u>

Please remember to SHARE if you find this useful! Appreciate you guys!

Coach Mace

How My Story Inspires Me to Inform You

I'll never forget the image of my dream school walking away from my High School spring practice. I wondered if I caught their attention. I wondered if there was any kind of chance. Standing at 5'9" on a good day, that chance was much less than I perceived at the time. Given that the average Division 1 Quarterback stands at roughly 6'2", I should have understood my weakness and its counterpart. At that time, Kyler Murray, standing half an inch taller, was committing to Texas A&M with D1 offers to spare. For me, performing well at one of the best schools in Oklahoma wasn't enough to counter my lack of height. Kyler Murray was able to beat the odds by having speed no one could match and winning 4 State Championships in the great state of Texas, a football powerhouse. There is so much more to the iceberg of College Football recruiting than 18-year-old kids can see. Most people think that making plays is good enough to gain the attention of a College Football Coach. It isn't. As a College Football Coach, I see where I missed back in the day. I have the eyes that my younger self wanted the attention of. I'm here to reveal that full iceberg to you.

I wish I could give the knowledge of recruiting I have now to my 14-year-old self. Now, I've been around coaches that recruit at every level. I played D2 football on a full scholarship, coached at a power 5 program, and assisted at another division 1 program. My knowledge of the process grows more and more each year. Although I can't send information back to 2013, I can do something even better; pass my knowledge to others and allow it to help you chase your dreams. So, the following will be very informational, and I pray that it assists you in your process. There's no guarantee that this book will get you to the next level. In the end, I can't put the work in for you. Limitations can only be broken by you.

Disclaimer: I'm giving you what I know. Certain opinions or advice may not be applicable for every program, but from where I have been and what I have experienced. I may not be the most qualified, but I promise you will get something out of this.

PART 1 >>>
UNDERSTANDING YOURSELF

Close the Gap!

THE GAP IS THE DISTANCE BETWEEN WHERE YOU ARE AND WHERE YOU WANT TO BE.

1. UNDERSTAND WHAT YOU WANT (EX: DIVISION 1 OFFER)
2. UNDERSTAND WHERE YOU ARE AT
3. CLOSE THE DISTANCE IN BETWEEN (CLOSE THE GAP)

Having a genuine understanding of your talent, skill level, school grades and football IQ in comparison to numbers of current Division 1 Athletes will help you understand the GAP in between... You cannot look at this from a skewed point of view. Your momma's opinion of you will not take you to the next level. **It is VITAL that you are REALISTIC about where your talent is.** Having all the confidence in the world is a good thing, but to get where we want to be, we must see where we are through a true lens. How is a College Football Coach looking at me right now? How do I compare to his players on his team?

GPA is another number that's important. Having a good GPA will open a lot more doors for you and having a bad GPA will close many doors you wouldn't expect... trust me, I've seen it.

Therefore, GPA should be something you are realistically looking at and trying to improve.

Being realistic about yourself is getting the most accurate numbers possible. Height, Weight, 40-yard dash, etc. all matter when evaluating yourself. And getting accurate numbers doesn't mean having your friend time you on his iPhone behind the Elementary school. It means going to camps, combines, running track, or participating in your school's offseason program that will **officially** get those numbers for you.

If you don't know the following measurements, then the first thing you need to do is to find them out as soon as possible. These are the three most looked at numbers by CFB Coaches before they watch you play.

It's a Game of Numbers

It's a NUMBER Game! Data is everything. Coaches will see your numbers before they see you. Most spreadsheets that coaches use to organize their recruits have the following, usually, in a similar order:

Graduation Year, Name, Position - Height // Weight // 40 Yard Dash // GPA

Some other numbers that might interest College Coaches:

Bench // Squat // Clean // Any track jumps or times // Arms strength (QB's) // Flexibility // Playing stats (Rushing Yards, Passing Yards, TD's, Tackles, Sacks, Forced Fumbles, etc.)

Therefore, before you get on any spreadsheet, you must know your numbers yourself. What does your spreadsheet say?

Because the numbers won't lie to you.

Once you have a realistic number of where you are at, the next step is seeing where you want to be.

1. **Look up your dream school and a few other schools you want to play at.**
2. **Look up the starting player that plays at your position.**
3. **Research / Write down his height, weight, 40 yard dash and any other numbers or stats you can find.**
4. **Watch his film from high school.**
5. **Compare.**

How do you feel after seeing that? Scratch that. It doesn't matter how you feel because that won't get you to that level. There is no pity when chasing your dreams. There's no time to feel hopeless. There is only time to work.

So do exactly that... You see the gap of where you are and where you want to be, so go close it.

If you don't see a gap, then don't get complacent. There are still some missing pieces if you aren't getting the offers or college interest. Your job is to find what that gap is.

Those stats are important, but **first and foremost, you must be making plays and putting it on film.**

The best athlete in the world can go without offers if he is not SEEN.

FYI... Unfortunately, this means that injuries will lower your chances of being seen. Take care of yourself and do your best at being on the field as much as possible.

WHAT'S MY WEAKNESS?

While you are still evaluating yourself, **it is important to find out what your weakness is.**

If an army is at war, the leaders know what the army's weakness is. It has to know in order to protect the army as a whole. If the weakness isn't something that the leader can change, he will overcompensate a strength to make up for the weakness.

That's exactly what you must do. Find your weakness. **If you can't change it, overcompensate that weakness with a strength.**

Height isn't something that we can just put the work in to change. Sure, sleep more, pray to

God, throw some salt in your shoes, and be healthy, but you can't always beat genetics by lifting more weight or working harder.

When I was in the 8th grade, Tim Tebow won the Heisman. I remember watching stories of him lifting and being a strong Quarterback. I strived to be like that. The problem was that I was overcompensating my lack of height with the wrong strength. Tim Tebow used his strength to compliment his height. My strength helped, but speed, as someone like Kyler Murray has proven, would have given me a better chance.

If you can't change it, **find a position where your weakness isn't a weakness.** A lot of times, guys get overlooked because of size, yet they are the best tackler on the team, and they're overlooked because they are 6'2' playing Defensive End. At a Linebacker position, they wouldn't be overlooked. Understanding yourself and having a sense of reality to what kind of people are getting recruited will benefit you in the long run of recruiting.

Once your weakness is understood, find a division 1 standout with a similar weakness, yet make plays despite that. Then find out WHY they are successful and HOW they battle that weakness. This is exactly what I should have done my high school days. I should have recognized my weakness was HEIGHT and overcompensated with SPEED.

It's your job to understand where you are at and what coaches are looking for then...

CLOSE THE GAP!!!

Handle Your Business.

This entire recruiting process is deep. You might be good enough. You might be getting the looks you want. But there's going to be so much more evaluated than just your football skill.

Listen to me very carefully, this process goes way beyond just football. I've seen guys get thrown off the recruiting board because of a bad handshake or because they mumble when they talk.

Sometimes, these things don't matter. Some coaches only care that you can play ball, listen, and pass just enough to get by in school. Most coaches will look for the best in every aspect of your life.

Your physical skill will get you the look, everything else will take the interest higher. Things like GPA, grades, character, social skills, conversation skills, family, your criminal record, your school discipline history, your speech, your extracurricular activities...

Questions will be asked like: Will he fit in here? How does he get along with the current

17

players? Is he smart? Does he talk good? Does he have good posture? Does he eat enough? Is he sloppy? What does he want to study? Does he seem to love football?

SCHOOL & GPA

I cannot emphasize enough how much your GPA will be talked about in recruiting / evaluation meetings. You must be eligible with your GRADES to be recruiting for your skill. This shows that you can handle a workload.

1. Find the schools you're interested in
2. Look for admissions information.
3. Compare your GPA to their preferred.
4. Any further questions, call the school counselor.
5. If you are in contact with a coach, talk to the coach about it

Make sure that you are enrolled in the NCAA eligibility center. This is easy. Just google it or ask your high school coach about it.

FAMILY MATTERS

Your family matters in this process. They matter in all levels. They're going through the process with you. If not your family, you have a close coach or guardian that should help you in the process. If not, find one or ask a high school coach.

For one, take their advice, but also, don't just do what they say. This is your decision. This is your life.

On another level...

They're in this with you. Don't think that coaches won't be watching how your parents will act too. Not to make things stiff for anyone, but everyone is being judge in these interactions. Coaches are being judged by prospects, prospects are being judged by coaches, and parents are being judged by coaches.

Parents, you're trusting this coach be the person who speaks the most words to him in his young adult life. Make sure you are guiding and leading your son in the process. You are also being judged by that coach. If you like him, make sure you are on your best behavior. Make sure you are pushing to find the most authentic version of that coach. Remember, he's being a salesman trying to get your kid to come play for him. At the end of the day, he wants to win. There are still genuine, good, caring coaches, but many get blinded by the money.

I've seen coaches hold offers from prospects because their father was too pushy. I've heard questions like: How tall is the dad? What do the parents think? Do the parents respond to texts? The Dad is a coach? The dad looks out of shape, do you think he will eat too much? The Mom seemed a little arrogant, what do you think?

Everyone is judging everyone else. The goal of these interactions is to find the GENUINE, REAL PERSON. Who am I doing business with here? How can I make sure that I am presenting myself in the very, best way?

Full transparency, college coaches want to win. They look at every single aspect and they get it from whoever they can talk to. They've done it a long time and they know what they're looking for.

Most people know the right way to do things. Your personal life is your business. You can't allow it to affect your football life.

If you think this amount of evaluating is bad, wait till NFL scouts start scouting you...

So... Handle Your Business!

Now, Separate from the Pack.

So, you closed the gap. Your skill is being evaluated and you're starting to gain some interest from schools you're interested in. You've handled your business off the field, and you are going to continue to do so...

What's next?

Separate from the pack!

By the way, the pack is **HUGE.** 1,028,761 students played high school football in 2023.

You've heard of this number game before, but it only gets worse as you incline in your college career. Only 7% make it to college ball and only 3% go Division 1.

Whatever school you're interested in, you MUST understand that you're chasing the impossible, so you're going to have to do what seems to be impossible. To be real with you, sometimes, even that isn't enough. But this dream inside you is worth finding out. Because every man or woman will ask this one question in their adult life; "Was I good enough?"

Time to find out.

You're gaining interest from colleges! Congrats. Still a long road ahead. Because, as we will discuss later. An offer isn't concrete anymore. Especially, these days with the transfer portal and NIL, your scholarship offer doesn't mean anything until you sign those papers.

How to separate from the pack is a whole other book, but you must be the most excellent version of yourself to give yourself the slightest chance of doing this thing.

This goal is important. You must push to be the best version of yourself. There is going to be disadvantages. There's always someone bigger, taller, faster, stronger, etc. There's always someone working harder than you. To separate from the pack, you can't get content. The more you rest, the further ahead someone else gets.

Even if you are working much harder than anyone at your school, remember about all the other kids around the state... around the country... with the same, exact dream as yours. Work harder!

PART 2 >>>
UNDERSTANDING THE PROCESS

Become Reachable

This is much more important than anyone might realize. For some reason, **Twitter** has become the networking source of every football coach in the nation. This is pretty well known by most players as they do a good job of using Twitter to showcase their football skills, attributes, and statistics. It might not be known to everybody.

Honestly, don't use your twitter for anything else other than football. You can afford to sacrifice a few years of a platform on social media just for football. If you don't have a Twitter, make one. This is purely for football reasons.

I know Twitter says, 'What's on your mind?" but don't tweet anything that is on your mind. MAYBE it's okay to tweet things that you know are APPROPRIATE, but don't risk anything else. Your tweets should purely be about football. And don't "favorite" anything that is inappropriate, because Twitter pulls that and puts it on your follower's page. You don't want people seeing things that are inappropriate that you favorited on their timeline.

Hype your team up all you want, but you must be careful retweeting your players highlights or stats. If you tweet too much of it, coaches might have trouble finding your highlights, film, stats, etc. You want coaches to pull your twitter up and find your film, stats, information, etc. (We will talk more about this later.)

Set up your profile the right way.

Your Twitter Profile, with an appropriate username, should display:

- Your legal name (If go by something different, put in quotations)
- A picture that shows your face (No helmet picture, you want people to be able to notice who you are if they saw you without a helmet in case they want to talk to you)
- Class
- Height / Weight / 40 Yard Dash (if it is good)
- Team you play for, Jersey Number, Positions
- Hudl highlight link needs to go into website or 247 Profile if one is made on you.
- Location

This setup makes scouting you much easier. They have everything they need right there.

When that offer comes through, POST IT! You want people to see that you were offered by a school. **Recruiters look at that**, so show it! Most players do a usual 2-3 Picture post and announce something about the school offering them. Many coaches will ask, "What's he got going?" Meaning who else has offered him. There are certain schools that an offer can really change the game for your recruiting, so advertise it.

You can post about a school's interest, I believe that adds value showing that you are on the radar for big schools, but don't over post that. You really want OFFER POSTS as it adds value to what other schools see in you. Sad to say, but a lot of schools are too lazy to recruit so they might go off who other schools are offering. You get on the radar of one school, you are bound to be on the radar for many other similar schools.

Go find coaches. This is a good resource to find coaches at different places. For the most part, coaches use Twitter more than they do email. Message them if you want. (More on communication later.)

Other social media should be used responsibly. I think it is common sense on how to use it appropriately. Coaches want to understand you as a person. Social media usage reflects you as a person. It displays how you act as a person. It could take away a possible scholarship. Assume a Coach will see everything you put out and post accordingly. You live in a world where it is rare that there isn't some form of a camera watching you: all phones, security cameras, doorbell cameras, video cameras, etc. If a Coach questions your character, they will try and find out what you do on that other side of the lens. BE RESPONSIBLE.

Set up a Google Drive with all your information. This can be an easy way to effectively share what you need to with any Coach very easily. Set up a Google Drive folder. Separate other folders in things like: Film link, additional film, drill work, transcripts, statistics, etc. If a Coach asks for any of that, you can send the link directly and a Coach will have all he needs. Add stuff to it if there are other areas that you find Coaches are asking for. If they ask for a film, always be straight forward and send your hudl link directly.

247 Sports Profile & Other Platforms

I don't know everything about what goes into getting a 247 Profile, but I know that it is a helpful thing. I believe that most guys will receive a 247 Profile when a D1 offer is given, or they are projected to be recruited highly. I think this is helpful to have so coaches can find you easily, but it might be something out of your control.

If you know someone that works for 247, it wouldn't hurt to ask them what it takes to get one. Some of the combine camps might offer possible 247 Profile opportunities. This and Rivals is really the only thing that Recruiters that I have worked with go off of any other company that promises to make a recruiting profile isn't doing anything more than making you a website like your Twitter. I think it helps to go to those kinds of camps, but not to overdue them.

All this to say, once that first D1 offer comes, your profile gets in front of multiple eyes. Most D1 Coaches will watch your film when a D1 school offers.

Get your skills in front of the right eyes.

Recruiting Periods

Recruiting periods change. You must understand when Coaches are **1. Able to talk to you 2. Actively Recruiting 3. Not available.**

Understanding this will allow you to strategically use your time in a more effective manner. Set the dates. Write down important dates in the recruiting world.

Coaches can talk to you at different times throughout the year. Not only does it depend on the time period, it depends on your class. There are sometimes when coaches can't talk to Freshmen-Sophomore but can talk to Junior-Seniors. Understanding this schedule will allow you to understand a Coach's interest.

As it gets even more complex, there are certain times coaches are limited in HOW they talk to you. Sometimes, they can openly communicate with you and sometimes they can't call you, but they can DM you on Twitter. Sometimes, there are times that you CAN call coaches and they can answer, but at the same time, they can't call you.

It gets complex when it comes to these rules. There are specific dates, but they constantly change. You can find these dates with an easy google search or talking to coaches about these periods. I don't want to give dates, and someone reads this years later to use it as a point of reference and they're all wrong. If a Coach is liking your pictures or sending notifications for you to notice, it wouldn't hurt to give them a call.

It's important to know when a Coach is busy in season. It doesn't hurt to try and reach out, but it is vital that you don't bother them when they are in season so bad that they block you or become annoyed with you. When it reaches that point, you take away credibility from yourself. Be professional.

Coaches will recruit during the spring after their team's spring ball practices. All of May is when Coaches will go out and truly try and see guys. A lot of the time this is at school spring practices or athletic periods.

I'll discuss means of communication later.

Summer Camps

Summer camps are tricky. I can give you my opinion, but this is where it is vital to understand where your skills stand and use the information at hand to best execute your summer plan.

Best case scenario, you never have to go to a summer camp. Coaches see your film as a freshman and you get the biggest offer, just like that. But that's so rare, I've never seen that personally. When you're young, go to summer camps. If you are wanting to gain interest, go to summer camps. It's good for you to see the amount of talent and quantity of players with the same dream as you. It will humble you and motivate you to work harder. See the gap, see the pack, work harder.

These camps all run differently.

I would advise you to reach out to schools you might want that aren't showing interest. Sometimes, schools believe they know players more than they do. Some schools won't even mess with players who have "ideal offers." For example, Wisconsin will probably not offer the Oklahoma division 1 recruit that has an offer from Oklahoma and Alabama. But if, for some reason, that division 1 recruit wants a

Wisconsin offer, it doesn't hurt to try and go out to summer camp at Wisconsin and earn that offer.

If you are entering summer with no offers on the level you are wanting. Go swing for the fences. You must understand several different things.

There is no guarantee.

Even if a Coach INVITES you to camp, that doesn't mean that you are up for an offer. It doesn't mean you will get an offer. I went to 6+ camps the summer before my senior year. I was given the best compliments by coaches all over camps. I was invited to most of them, and I didn't receive an offer at any of the camps. Most kids will not earn an offer on spot. I've been part of camps where they offer 3-5 kids on spot and part of camps where no one was offered anything. Just because you show up and ball out, it doesn't earn you a scholarship. There are layers to this business.

There are different types of camps.

MEGA Camps are camps with large quantities of players and many different schools coming to watch. These camps will (usually) consist of measuring height, weight, 40 yards dash, and sometimes, broad jump, L Drill, Shuttle drill, bench, and vertical jump. They will go into position drills, group work, and then 1on1s. To earn the eyes of the host, you must show out. Sometimes, you will be put off because of your size. That's fine! There are still other schools at these camps that are watching. Impress them and open your options.

At these MEGA Camps, you need to network prior. Find out what schools are going to be there and reach out to them. Have your head Coach reach out to them. Then go ball out.

I would not spend all my camp dates going to Mega Camps. I would try one and then move on to schools that are interested or could be interested.

Other camps include your regular Elite Camps at schools all over. These MIGHT consist of similar tests. They will consist of position work and some form of competition. These are tricky as it might change for different schools. Sometimes schools might have an elite camp, yet have hundreds of players out making it tough to get reps. Some schools have less people and can truly scout out the skill.

Every little thing the Coaches SEE matters.

This varies for every coach, but you must realize how much is at stake with every drill, every rep, and every second. Even social aspects are important to some coaches. If you are somewhat of a baller, but they don't like the way you handle yourself socially, then you're scratched off the list.

You must realize that a Coach can't see every rep you take. You can't control or know which rep they are watching. You must assume it is every rep that a coach sees and executes each rep.

Do not wear a brace if you don't need it. Now, let me make it clear, wear a brace if the doctor tells you to! No question. Wear it. But if you have a brace that you self-diagnosed yourself, it's a walking red flag to coaches. As unfortunate as it is, injuries are something coaches look at with caution. So be careful what you wear.

Most coaches have an understanding of who is there.

Especially, at small camps, Coaches know who is coming and will have seen your film prior to the camp. Some guys will get an idea of you from what your high school Coach says. I've seen guys with horrible films change the mind of important coaches making decisions on who to offer. At the camp you're at, it doesn't matter. All that matters is how you perform at the camp. Be the best in your group. Be the best at your camp.

Players will sometimes be separated.

Some camps will split you up depending on who they want to see. If this is the case, scout the other players out and understand what group is being scouted more. You want to know where the position coach is always going and be with him. Don't be annoying but get yourself in front of the right eyes.

Have some fun!

You only get to do these kinds of camps a few years out of your life. You will miss getting the opportunity to compete. Having fun will ease your nerves and allow you to showcase your true talent.

I'm hesitant on how much camp advice I want to give. Sometimes they work and sometimes they don't. Depending on the staff, they are all different. Dig for as much information as you can get and use information to make the right decision.

After each camp, take pictures with the Position Coach and Head Coach if given the opportunity. Post them on Twitter and thank them for their help.

WHO You Know Matters

This might be one of the most important things you can do: NETWORK. Meet people. Meet football people and have them vouch for you. By the way, this is important beyond football. This is advice you can take beyond the yard markers.

Your Head Coach is the most important person in your network. Some Head Coaches do GREAT at recruiting and even have specific coaches on staff handle a lot of it. Some coaches are the absolute worst and can't even give us names of their players. BUT either way, he is still the most important person in your network.

Every college coach I have known will check with the high school coach before offering just anybody. The Head Coach gives solid words and College Coach offers. Not only that, but IF the Head Coach recommends anybody, a College Coach will look if he trusts the High School coach's word. Most do.

The most important thing to do with this is to make sure your High School Coach knows what YOU want to do. If you want to play at any level, let him know. If you would want to walk on at a division 1 school, let him know. It is vital that the Head Coach knows what you want, because he holds the key to your future. Make sure you make your high school coach a priority when deciding where to spend your time. Summer 7v7 can be fun, but if your coach wants you working there, be there. You want your Head Coach happy because he will be contacted by college coaches.

Your position coach is important too. Not only will he teach you important skills, but he might have a connection to people he knows. I receive calls from position coaches advocating for their players all the time. I'll watch their film if that is the case.

Each person you know has their own network of people they know. In the football world, connections are EVERYTHING. Not only do you need to meet these people, but you need to LEARN from these people and make them WANT to represent you by working hard and impressing them.

Train with trainers who have connections. They can sometimes have a word in the college football world. You must understand their relations and make sure you are not paying someone just to send DMs to random coaches on Twitter. You can do that yourself. But check to see who they know and who their network really is before spending any money.

It is so easy to see who people know with social media these days. Checking who follows people and who they follow back. It doesn't always mean they know them, but it is likely! **UTILIZE SOCIAL MEDIA TO SEE PEOPLE'S NETWORKS.**

Honestly, just talk to people. It doesn't hurt you to reach out and be a friendly person. It doesn't hurt you to try and get to know all the people you meet. Knowing people is your ladder through today's world. Most people that get anywhere have used that ladder to become where they are today.

Film

This is one of the more important things you need in this process. You need to have plays on tape. I'll probably repeat this a lot in this book, but it all doesn't mean anything if you don't have plays on tape. So here are my tips on film:

Use Hudl. Coaches are looking for a bird's eye view of your game. They aren't looking for sideline views and cool edits and everything like that. You can post that, but don't use that as the film you send to recruiters. Hudl is your go to. Set up your Hudl and make sure your profile is findable. Put your full name in it. Set it up through your high school so coaches can find you on the Hudl roster. If you go by something else, put your preferred name in the middle with parentheses. EX (Deondre "De De" Brooks). Put your CORRECT height and weight in your profile (you don't want to lie just for a Coach to see that in person.) At the beginning of the slides, put your **NAME, HEIGHT/WEIGHT, MUGSHOT PICTURE, CLASS, CONTACT INFORMATION AND POSITION** in the beginning slide. You can put your stats or recognition (like All-State, All-District, etc.) in the next slide, but you don't want too many slides taking up the time a Coach has where he could be watching you play.

Circle yourself before the play starts. My advice would be to not use any other shape besides a circle. When editing, you'll see what I mean by that. There are a lot of nonsense tools you can circle yourself before the play. A lot of them take too much time. It's best to do a circle to show exactly who you are in a quick, efficient way. This doesn't mean coaches won't watch. If you are making plays, then coaches will watch.

Circle **BEFORE THE PLAY**. This is important because you want coaches' eyes on you the entire time. If a play is going on and a circle isn't placed prior to the snap of the ball, a coach will have no idea where to look for you (unless you are a Quarterback or something, but I would still circle).

Understand what coaches are looking for with your position. This is all up to your position. You must place your plays in an order that will CATCH & HOLD a Recruiter's attention. It can't be at random. What's your best, mind blowing play? Put it at the front. Then follow with plays that prove your worth at that position.

I can't tell you what is important to each Coach, but I'll mention a few things that are important to each position below:

Quarterback: Arm strength, accuracy, pocket movement, athleticism

Running Back: Quickness, speed, cuts, flexibility

Wide Receivers: Speed, hands, cuts, quickness

Offensive Line: Strength, Pulls/Speed, flexibility, run blocking, pass blocking.

Defensive Line: Quickness, hand usage, violence, sacks

Linebackers: Tackle ability, reading offensive line, flexibility, speed

Defensive Backs: Speed, agility, route tracking, coming downhill to tackle.

Ask the coaches you know who specialize in the position to help you with what other things to include. You want a mix of all of these throughout your film. Don't sort it by each thing but mix it and put your best clips at the beginning.

Know when to cut. You must understand that you have about 5 plays to keep a coach's interest. I can't tell you how many times "Okay I've seen enough" is thrown around in the film room while recruiting. Therefore, you must be efficient when it comes to cutting plays. Keep what is necessary and cut extra stuff. You might look cool calling an audible as a Quarterback, but don't keep that in your film. Start it right before you snap it. Defensive players can cut it a few seconds before the snap, so coaches can see how you are moving pre-snap.

No slow motion. No music. Depending on the staff, coaches won't want music, because they'll be in a large meeting room discussing what they are seeing. Slow motion takes up time and Coaches don't like any kind of time being altered. Speeding up is lying about your speed and slowing down doesn't help a coach's perspective as he sees the game at full speed 100% of the time. Trust me, if he wants to see something again, he will rewind it.

EARN THEIR ATTENTION. There aren't a lot of tricks to film. You either have what it takes or not. If you aren't putting plays on tape, then you aren't proving to coaches that you have what it takes. Your number one job is to make plays. There isn't a lot of way around that. Coaches will watch your film if they are recruiting you and if you aren't earning their attention, then they won't care. They have way too much on their plate to worry about kids that don't have good film. Your craft matters. Perfect it and show that on film.

A Coach's Process

A Coach's process is a tough subject because there are so many ways, strategies, and habits that coaches have picked up over the years.

I'll give everything I've seen and touch on some stuff I've heard of coaches doing. First, we will touch on a football staff later on. This chapter, I want to just talk about the **position coach**. The position coach is the one recruiting you. I'll explain his whole year and what his process is and try to organize it in the best way possible.

I think it's important to note that recruiting is a long, tiring part of the job for college coaches. A lot of people dislike being on the road, away from family for a month when the season already takes up most of their time. That is why recruiting can be kind of sloppy for some coaches.

Position Coach + Position Manager "A position coach is the head coach of his position." Majority of programs, the position coach is handling personnel of their position. He decides who gets offered. But the bigger the school, the more help they have with each position. Knowing this, you can emphasize who you try and reach out to. Emailing or messaging the TE Quality Control Coach over a DB position isn't going to help you, much. Find the guys that work in your position for the school you're interested in and hit them up!

Once again, it's all about numbers. To be real, coaches only have a certain number of recruits they can truly take. That's why a position coach is the manager of his position. He has to manage the number of guys he has in his room, who is leaving, who is coming, and who he is recruiting. Keep in mind, the transfer portal has made this much more complex for high school recruits. Because that has to play into the number of guys at the position as well. We will hit on the portal later on.

A Coach's Year in Recruiting

Let's start the year in the beginning of the school year / season. August. I think it's good to see how coach's move through the season / off-season so you understand where things happen and why.

Fall / Season (August - November)

A Coaches busiest season. He will be in at 7am and leave the office at 10pm for the average CFB Coach. His schedule is full, but he will still recruit and do a good job at it. Most of this recruiting is over the phone with some possible game visits on the coaches bye weeks or local high schools.

Unofficial visits will happen. Official Visits will happen. Recruits will receive plenty of graphics and will be asked to come to as many games as possible. Coaches try and keep up with recruits season and stay in touch with you as much as possible.

Winter / Post-Season Bowls (December - January)

Recruiting gets narrow here. Obviously, Coaches are trying to finalize their commitments for the first signing day in December with the Seniors, so that will be the final shot at some of their recruits. You have two signing days at this time. One in December and one in February (this will change and has changed before).

The Coaches will go recruit for a period of time in January / December. BUT They will be out of contact and on vacation from around Christmas time to the New Years. Depending on the recruiting calendar they may be responsive, or they may not.

The Transfer Portal opens from late December to early January.

Spring / Off-season

Spring workouts start and the team has majority of the players that will be with them for the spring session. Some early high school enrollees may role in and some portal guys may be added. Spring Ball will start around February - May with 15 possible practice dates that recruits are able to visit, unofficially.

May will be full of coaches being on the road. They will be on the road for the full month and recruiting mode will be full swing.

The Portal Opens from April 15 - April 30.

Summer / Eval Season

Summer happens and Coaches will get a break from work around Memorial Day at the end of May, then be back in office and working with some OTAs on campus for the month of June.

June = a lot of summer camps and recruiting becomes hot. A lot of evaluations mixed with Official visits on the weekends or during the week.

47

July is a coaches vacation and he will be out all of that month. Dead period, so recruiting won't be hot till the last week of July when some camps open back up.

Summer / Recruiting & Vacation

June is HOT for recruiting. A lot goes down and you, as a recruit, will be busy as well. **Summer Camps** happen and this is big for recruiting. I'll touch more on Summer Camps and you're perspective on it later, but just know that coaches do use these camps for recruiting and it's not always some money grabber. **Official Visits** will happen more starting this year because of the earlier signing date. So schools will have Official Visits happening all summer.

There is some time period early in the summer where coaches can't talk to Junior, but only Seniors. Don't let that upset you if no one his hitting you back, they're just not allowed to. Check the recruiting calendar.

A Coach's Organization of Prospects

By Your Graduation Year

Coaches will organize their recruits and evaluations by CLASS or GRAD YEAR. Your high school graduation class is how you will be recruited. Starting with the most urgent... at this period it's 2025's. To the next urgent, 2026's. And on to 2027's and 2028's. You won't see much recruiting out of the 2027's and 2028's so no worries if you're not getting much traction, but you really want to start getting recruited as a High School Junior. This means, best case scenario, you need some film to show from your sophomore year. No worries if not, but the more time you play in high school, the higher chance you'll have of being seen.

By Skill Level

This is where it gets tricky. A lot of coaches have their own system. They have the evaluate hundreds of players, every month. SO, the best way to organize their thoughts are by organizing their prospects. BUT each school can't just recruit the very best player, because the very best players go to the very best programs. So different programs will wither down their list of how they rank players, and it helps the coaches evaluate and organize their thoughts moving forward.

Some of the places I have been organize recruits in the following way:

0: National - This is usually for smaller schools that don't have a shot of recruits that are getting recruited by bigger schools but want to stay in touch with the recruit just in case he enters the portal later on.

A: Offer / Top Guy: Top Guys are the guys the coach of the position wants the most. Someone that a coach would honor a scholarship for if the player decided to commit. These are the guys that the coach believes has a chance of landing and that can for sure help the team. These guys will be asked to come on an official visit as well as unofficial visits.

B: Offer / Hold: Sometimes, a coach will throw an offer at a player and keep him in mind as a back up plan. That sounds bad, but the player still has an offer. The hold means that it's not a committable offer at that moment. These guys will be asked to come on an unofficial visit, and possibly an official visit.

C: Walk On: Usually, these interactions come later after signing day, but that is how coaches will label recruits if they are not what they are looking for at this time. These guys will be asked to come to camp and work with the coach or will be asked after signing day to come visit.

D: Can't play here: This is exactly what it sounds. If a Coach puts this label on a prospect, then he will probably not recruit you or talk to you outside of a camp.

Some other key words include:

Top Guy: This means you are on the board. It means that you are a guy the coach is recruiting heavy, will probably want to be on a Official Visit, and an offer is committable.

Prospect: An eligible high school player that the coach is checking out, but not yet actively recruiting.

Recruit: An eligible high school player that a coach is actively recruiting or trying to persuade to commit.

OV or Official Visit: Official Visit is a visit for Top Recruits that is paid for by the school / team. On these visits, the sky is the limit. Photoshoots, a lot of food, activities, hotel, and hanging out with the current team happens. This is only allowed on certain periods in the recruiting process.

Unofficial Visit: Nothing is allowed to be paid for by the coach / school. It has to be on campus or within one mile of campus. This is what coaches will try and have initial in person interactions with prospects. It also allows the recruit to see the school or practice and how everything operates.

Recruiting Periods

Now, Coaches have different recruiting periods for different classes that allows that coach the ability to contact, evaluate, or see in person recruits or evaluations.

Contact period: is that period of time when it is permissible for authorized athletics department staff members to make in-person, off-campus recruiting contacts and evaluations.

An **evaluation period** is that period of time when it is permissible for authorized athletics department staff members to be involved in off-campus activities designed to assess the academic qualifications and playing ability of prospective student-athletes. No in-person, off-campus recruiting contacts shall be made with the prospective student-athlete during an evaluation period.

A **dead period** is that period of time when it is not permissible to make in-person recruiting contacts or evaluations on or off the member institution's campus or to permit official or unofficial visits by prospective student-athletes to the institution's campus.

A **quiet period** is that period of time when it is permissible to make in-person recruiting contacts only on the member institution's campus. No in-person, off-campus recruiting contacts or evaluations may be made during the quiet period.

DISCLAIMER: This is a COACH'S process. This means you won't always get their information on this. Unfortunately, It also means that you might hear one thing from him and it doesn't always mean that he's telling the truth.

Communication

Communication is vital when it comes to recruiting!

Another tricky subject because coaches aren't always allowed to talk to prospects. It's important to know when coaches can talk to you and when they can't. I mentioned some of the recruiting periods in the previous lesson that include contact period, evaluation period, etc. I'll attach a recruiting calendar at the end, so you can see how things operate on the calendar year for recruiting.

Like mentioned before, make sure you are reachable. If you have a common name like "John Smith," make sure you are putting enough football related content on your twitter to ensure that the search bar can find you. Include your position and school in almost everything.

Twitter communication - this will be your main line of conversation until you become someone the coach wants to recruit. Open them DMs Up!!!! & respond fast. It might even be a good idea to keep your phone number in your Twitter bio if you're okay with that private info being out.

Phone communication - this will be your go to as you become a recruit for a coach and are on his list of guys to recruit. Texting, phone calls, and facetime calls are all coming your way. Answer them! Reply ASAP. Not the end of the world if it takes you a minute, but good to be responsive when need be.

Other possible forms of communication - I've seen some other stuff that might happen. Some coaches want to work their way around rules so they keep it on the down low. They might try and communicate through XBOX / PS5 parties or snapchat. Whatever it might be, it might happen so don't be taken off by it. They just want to try and build relationships with you.

TAKE THE PHONE OFF DO NOT DISTURB. This seems to be a major trend right now where guys like to keep their phone without notifications, I get that, but some conversations don't come around all that often. If you get a chance to talk to a big time coach, you want to take it. Don't miss opportunities.

SIDE NOTE: You might be getting recruited big time, but don't neglect some coaches at smaller levels. Talk to them too, but don't waste time! Why? Because that Division 2 Coach might just end up being an Offensive Coordinator at a Power 5 school the next year. If you ghost him, he is going to do the same to you. Just be communicative about your situation and what you're thinking. Replying like "Hey Coach! I appreciate your interest. Would love to stay in touch, but I am shortening might focus to a few Power 5 schools at this time. ALSO, you might hit this thing one day that's called THE TRANSFER PORTAL so keep your relationships in good standing.

(You might be like me and want to get into coaching so good recruiting relationships now, might help good working relationships later.)

What's an Offer?

Nothing Matters till You Sign an NLI

An offer doesn't mean what I always thought it meant. A Coach isn't bound to honor an offer. He's not bound to honor a commitment either (Another reason why you should keep your lines of communication with other coaches open).

You are in the same boat. You aren't bound to your commitment. You can flip and open back up your recruitment. I would advise that you treat coaches how you would want to be treated but look after what is best for you first. You don't want to burn any bridges.

What's an NLI?

Not to get you confused with NIL (Name Image Likeness) - **NLI is National Letter of Intent.** This letter shuts down all recruiting and you are now to be honored as a future enrollee / player. Hold these rules loosely because they may change in the future. It doesn't apply to Transfer Portal recruits. Portal recruits are only bound to a school when they attend their first class on campus.

IF YOU GET AN OFFER-

There are a lot of ways to handle this, but it's good to:

1. Post it on Twitter. The bigger the school, the more clout you will start to get. This is you advertising your talents. Unfortunately, recruiting is more about chasing guys with offers than it is finding players who can play.

Hate to say this, but it's best for you to advertise what you want to be instead of what you get. If you think you're Division 1, don't post your offers till you get a Division 1 offer. This won't really hurt your chances, but when a coach sees a lot of D2 offers on your Twitter, he's going to label you in his head as a D2 player and might just skip over you (bad recruiting I know!).

When you get a Group of 5, D1 offer, others will start to come in hot. The biggest challenge is getting the first one. The truth is when you get an offer from one school, all the other similar schools will take a look at you. Take advantage of the clout.

2.Start studying the school / football team- Who is this coach? Where did he come from? What's his record? What kind of offense

or defense do they run? What's the depth chart looking like? School look like? Main thing to find out: DO I WANT TO PLAY HERE?

3.Stay in touch with the coaches you want to play for- I would start a notes page on your phone and label all your offers in order of what you are interested in most at the front. Put the coaches name next to it and hit the coach up. Coaches love this! It shows that you are interested and can communicate well.

Other topics- (I will add as they come up)

You can ask if an offer is committable, but the reality is that you will be able to tell from the process of the relationship with the coach. If you're getting plenty of attention, then yes, it more than likely is. If the coach is asking when you plan on committing then that's probably a good sign too.

PART 3 >>> UNDERSTANDING COLLEGE FOOTBALL PROGRAMS

A College Football Staff

Buckle Up!

Alright, let's jump into this thing. This complex business of College Football. This will be a lot to unpack, so buckle up and take some notes.

The College Football staff is different than anything else you've ever seen in your life. And it is different everywhere. Titles mean different things at one spot as it does another. There are layers to different departments of a college football team.

There is a ton of money in college football. There is a ton of passion in college football. Money + Passion = Competition. A "Whatever it takes" mentality is heavy in the offices of college football teams around the world.

The thing is that a lot of titles don't really mean anything. It might just be a way the Head Coach gets people more of a bump in their pay.

Note that the level of staff varies depending on the size of the school. This is a general Division 1 staff.

The President of the College & the Athletic Director

Let's start at the top. These guys have the overall say when it comes to who is hired as the head coach. The President hires the Athletic Director. The Athletic Director hires the Head Coach, maybe some others within football, but that's where a lot of his decision-making stops. The Athletic Director has a big job and a lot of sports, so even though football brings in most of his revenue, he stays away from most of the minor, semi major decisions when it comes to football. At some places, he might not have much control over the head coach. Depends on the clout of the Head Coach.

The Head Coach

The king of the program. This is the hero of it all. College Football doesn't have guys that stick around longer than 4 years, so the head coach gets a lot of victory praise if the program is good and performs.

The Head Coach has the decision making for everything. It is up to the Head Coach what happens at every major and minor decision. If he wants to let someone else take over the decisions for the minor issues, he is the one that appoints them. The Head Coach has very little supervision and can operate however he wants to operate.

The Head Coach MIGHT run the offense or defense if he feels like that's best for the team. He may hire someone he believes is better. Most of the time, the Head Coach is heavily involved on one side of the ball and hires a coordinator that he trusts to run the other side of the ball.

The Head Coach has final say on offers and roster changes. Usually, the head coach stays out of the way of coaches recruiting and will let the position coaches do their thing. Like I've said, it is a good thing if the Head Coach is heavily involved in your recruiting.

Associate Head Coach

This Coach is the next in line when it comes to decision making. This is a position coach, coordinator, it doesn't really matter, but usually is someone that is more of a veteran coach and someone the head coach trusts in decision making.

Coordinators

The next in line of this power ladder. Coordinators vary when it comes to responsibility. A lot of the times, the head coach might want to be the coordinator, but the appoint another to have the title for whatever reason it may be.

A lot of the times, the Head Coach gives the coordinators free reign to build their offense / defense in whatever way they decide. So, the coordinators might have more of a word into the decision making with the position coaches. Just like it's a good thing if the Head Coach is heavily involved in your recruiting, if the coordinator is

SIDE NOTE: You might have Run Game / Pass Game coordinators that have more responsibility as well.

**Position Coach

This is YOUR guy. He is the point leader in recruiting you. He is the one that wants you on the team and this is the guy you want to impress. Obviously, you want to impress the others, but the Position Coach is the one who's making the board and will make an argument for you to be recruited or not.

I've hit on the importance of your relationship with this coach, but I will emphasize it again.

This is a double-sided relationship. You should be recruiting this coach too.

Some position coaches might have recruiting areas and if that's the case, then it is important to build a relationship with him too. He will run point in a lot of your recruiting. But I would say it is a red flag if he is talking to you and the position coach of your position isn't (unless you're being recruited for multiple positions or as an athlete).

Graduate Assistants & Quality Control Coaches

Every position coach in Division 1 college football more than likely has a graduate assistant or a Quality Control Coach that works as the position coach's direct assistant. At a lot of programs, this will be who you hear from the 2nd most. He is the one that more than likely evaluated your film first and pushed you (the prospect) to the position coaches.

This guy does a lot of work for the coach. He does everything from getting film together to getting him coffee. He will be the one running around getting golf carts, assisting with food on visits, and helping you out a lot. He will also be the one you watch a lot of film with personally, ask more direct questions too and be able to talk to about some more personal stuff since he is a younger guy.

Football Operations

A football team will have a Director of Football Operations or Chief of Staff. These guys assist in all things football operations. They do a lot of background work. In your world, they will be the one that might assist you in dorm / living situations, meal plans, upon other things.

Recruiting Department

This will be another department that will heavily be involved in your recruiting process. There will be a Director of Recruiting, On Campus Recruiting Coordinator, Recruiting Coordinator, and some Scouting of Talent bosses. They will all have student workers or graduate assistants that will all help in the process. At bigger schools, these are the guys you will probably talk to the most.

Some Position Coaches at bigger schools have a team of: A Graduate Assistant (assisting in football), a Recruiting Assistant, an On Campus Recruiting Assistant. All work together in different aspects of recruiting your talent, finding out more information about your interests, and all building relationships to assist you and your communication with the position coach.

Strength Staff

Out of the football coaching staff, this is the most important person you should get to know as you go through the recruiting process. The 2 people that will help you and spend the most time with you in your college career is the position coach and the Head Strength Coach.

The Head Strength Coach has a team of around 3 depending on the school. He will be your guy who is with you in developing you as an athlete all summer. He will be with you all season, and when the position coaches are out recruiting. He is your guy that YOU need to recruit. You must develop as an athlete in the 4-5 years you are at a program.

Academics

Football will have an academic team that will assist in all things school. Usually, they class check, send out tutors, schedule your classes, and make sure you are on track.

Equipment

Equipment will have 2 guys that usually assist in all thing's equipment. Helmet, shoulder pads, knee braces, etc. Good to know this guy and make friends. He might throw you a couple extra shirts if you make good friends.

Medical Staff

The medical staff will have a little more power to overturn decisions by the head coach as they must be sure to protect you when the coaches might push you to your limits.

Prehab is important because it helps prevent injury. Rehab in the face of injury is important to get you back on the field. You will complete with the medical staff. They consist of Team Doctors, Dentists, Physical Therapists, Chiropractors, etc.

All these people working together to push you to be the best possible athlete you can be. Don't take it for granted, take advantage of the help when the time comes. You must make sure these teams you take note of as you get recruited.

In order:

1. Position Coach
2. Head Coach
3. Strength Coach
4. Everyone Else

New Age College Football

New Age College Football = The Wild Wild West

New rules, new opportunities to gain fortune, new opportunities to win. The rich get richer, and the poor get stolen from in the transfer portal from big schools waving big money.

These rules will continue to change as the years go on. They will change fast, so don't hold on too tightly to this information. Keep yourself updated on rules of College Football and stay informed.

NIL and the Transfer Portal being introduced the same year really made a dent in college football. It affected high school recruiting, hit small schools hard, and is really all a "try by trial" basis.

Please comment as we go, because I will dump as much information as I can and try and organize it the best possible way, but if anything seems muddy, please let me know and I will try and clear the waters.

Transfer Portal

I'm taking a deep breath as I dive into this fire...

The Transfer Portal... CFB Free Agency

So, I'm going to attack this like you haven't heard about this before ever. This didn't exist in the past. When I was a player in college, I would of used this. It's awesome for current players. It gets abused by some players, but for a guy that doesn't fit into a program, a chance to find a home that suits him is big time. For a walk on that took a chance on himself, got playing time, and earned a scholarship at another school, it's a dream come true.

The **Transfer Portal** is a tool that can be used by **current college football players** to enter into a pool of players that can **be recruited** by other schools and **transfer without penalty.**

This changes the game... & it can be dangerous.

The Negative Side

For High School Recruits:

Back in the day, transferring cost players a year of eligibility. That's no longer the case with the transfer portal. Because of this, schools are actively recruiting players that are currently playing college football. If coaches are recruiting current players, that opens the door for players that are not just ready to play in college but have experience on a college football team. So, this means that High School recruits are getting less recruited.

Unfortunately, this has been a bad affect for high school recruits. They aren't getting recruited by as big of schools previously or they are getting dropped for transfer portal players that the coaches believe can help the team win NOW rather than later. This has helped smaller schools because they are landing bigger high school recruits.

In the 2019 season, just 6.4% of FBS rosters were made up of transfers, according to data from SportSource Analytics. That number grew to 20.5% of rosters in 2023" (ESPN)

For Guys Who Hit the Portal

There is no guarantee that you will be picked up.

As soon as you hit the portal, there is a chance you will be lost in it. The numbers are SCARY. 2,400 players hit the portal last year. Only 1,900 found a home. 500 players got lost in the portal. The thing is that as soon as you hit the portal, your team does not have to take you back. That's why it is important to talk with your head coach about situation and what you decided to do.

Another Way of "Cutting"

Cutting is not allowed when it comes to skill level in College Football. Until you graduate with an undergrad or your eligibility expires, you are on that team.

If you hit the portal, you can be cut. A lot of coaches might disguise the portal as a means to get rid of players and open up a slot to bring someone else in. Be aware. Be smart. If they are trying to cut you, it's probably best you try and find another home, but do so in a way that is beneficial to you. Go talk to your high school coach. Get his help in finding a new home.

Tampering

Nick Saban said himself that he had a list of guys that were current college football players that he would offer. There are now lists at almost any college of current college football players that they are interested in taking. This means that tampering is more than likely happening. Tampering is the act of illegally recruiting guys that are current college football players.

Guys will get hit up after the season by bigger schools about hitting the portal so they can be recruited by them. This is bad business, but like I said, coaches will do whatever it takes to win. Bigger schools are stealing from smaller schools and utilizing NIL to recruit. More bad business. But keep in mind that it is happening. This might be good for certain players but hurts the business overall. Be smart when talking to coaches when you are on a current football team. You don't want to be caught in the middle of that.

The Positive Side

I believe there is more positive than negative when it comes to the player. You must play your cards right and be smart about the situation. You can't just leap and pray that you're caught. The #1 thing is to communicate with EVERYONE around you. Get advice from you position coach, your head coach, your family, people that are not involved with the program who have experience in your field, everyone! Sadly, you should take your coaches point of view on the subject with a grain of salt as they are looking out for themselves.

You Might Find the Perfect Spot

With all the selling that coaches and schools try to do, you might find yourself in a sea of lies that were promised by the coaches. The Head Coach told me that there would be a new football field 10 years ago at the school I committed to. They still play at the field I played on at that university. Not a big deal, but you will have to look past the fluff / exaggeration of the truth that coaches might sell. They aren't just coaches, they're salesman.

Beyond that, you might find a spot that fits you better. It might be a better system, it might be a coach you fit with better, it might be a better school overall, it might be a place that give you playing time and a better shot at the NFL.

You Might Find a Second Chance

Maybe you had a fallout with a previous school. Maybe bridges were burnt at your previous school. Maybe the school brought in someone else at your position that you don't see yourself beating out. The portal gives players a second chance at college football. Whatever mistakes were made, whatever unfortunate event that happens, it gives players a chance at the game that they deserve. Take advantage of the opportunity.

The Most Important Thing is PLAYING TIME

Don't chase the money. If you have a shot at the NFL, please do not chase the money. If there's a situation where you know that you won't play in the NFL and a possible paycheck might lead to setting you up now, then go for it.

The NFL money is DIFFERENT. When you are in the NFL and can compete, the benefits on the tail end are much better than that small NIL check that some schools are promising. The more playing time and chances you get to prove your worth in the NFL, take it.

A Hot Take on the Portal

Take this for what you want, I'm not saying this is the way to approach things. I'm not saying that this will always apply. In my opinion, I believe that coming out of high school, you should go to a place that you find the most playing time. You should try and earn your degree in 3 years, then go chase the money at a bigger school as a Graduate. This allows you to get film, gain confidence, then go play at a bigger spot and get that experience at a higher level.

If you are a top, Power 5 recruit... go big.

I do believe that you need to shoot for Division 1 if you are a division 1 player. The jump from D2 to D1 is near impossible. You can always jump to D2 from D1 and there's a better chance of taking a jump at a higher D1 from a smaller D1 than a top D2 program.

PLEASE ASK QUESTIONS... I KNOW I'M MISSING SOMETHING!

Name Image Likeness (NIL)

NIL = Name Image Likeness

NIL changes the game. Anything that money touches make everything much more complicated. I believe that NIL is needed, just like the portal, but it muddies the waters of College Football.

Money and the NCAA is already a very complex, layered issue. There are books written on this subject of paying athletes. I could write a whole book on this alone, but I don't want to waste your time with information that's not needed. Let me try to simplify...

TAKE NOTE: This will change every month. I will continue to update as it goes. New rules will hit every month, so keep yourself informed.

Overview

So, Name Image and Likeness is a law set in place that allows student athletes to be paid for their Name Image and Likeness. That could mean jersey sales, Instagram ads, shooting a local commercial, anything from a company outside of the University that's willing to pay the athlete.

As of right now (June 4, 2024), Student Athletes are not getting paid by the university. This would re-classify the status of amateurism with the NCAA and technically make these athletes "professional." The label of professional would alter the entire NCAA because most of the money that college athletics brings in is from College Football (except for March Madness in basketball).

This money that College Football brings in funds the entire athletic department, including sports that are in the negative. So, take away College Football funds and many other sports will suffer. The colleges may suffer too. So, this change could really affect college athletics if not done correctly. There are different angles of this. Opinions don't matter, just how this affects recruiting.

NIL and Recruiting

At this current moment, it is illegal to utilize NIL in recruiting. There may be secret ways around this, I just don't know them. What I do know is that schools will utilize NIL in recruiting. With collectives and other set-in stone programs, schools feel confident enough in the amount of money that is awarded.

The problem these teams are running into is that they are promising money and not coming through with the offer. Most of this money is situational and by the semester. It can even be decided within the semester. I've seen some promised funds being held because the student athlete wasn't performing academically. This means that someone has power to block those funds that are talked about. There's no solid contract in place, so what's promised isn't promised. Look these situations up in the news and you will find a lot of lawsuits happening right now against schools that promised funds.

This can be a great tool for players to be recruited. To make the money you deserve is exactly what NIL is intended to do. I think it is a great rule that players deserve. Take advantage of it where you can. Save it. Let the school pay for what you need, work hard, and use that money to buy a house or something later on in your life. The scholarship will cover everything you need plus more. Be smart with your money. It goes fast.

NIL hurts smaller schools

We've hit on this before, but smaller schools on all levels will lose out on recruits because of the promised NIL money for recruits from bigger schools. Some schools will even offer a walk on position but compensate the scholarship with

NIL money. This, technically, brings more scholarships available to schools that can afford it.

Other Money

Cost of Attendance

Schools are allowed to give scholarship players the remaining cost of attendance to compensate for food and living. Each scholarship player on the Division 1 level is given a monthly stipend. This number is different depending on the school size, funds, situation, and classification, but understand that this is another thing to ask about.

Other Funds Dependent on Schools

Some schools qualify for a pool of funds that can be distributed by the Head Coach but must be backed by academics. Some schools have funds that are donated by many different individuals that can be used for skillsets. These rules are all over and I don't know enough about them to touch on, but it is good to know that you can ask about other funds that you can earn on recruiting meetings with coaches.

Don't Let Money Be the Deciding Factor

Everyone's situation is different, but this money isn't money to bet on. It's very shaky and unreliable promise of money. If your situation is like all others and you want to and have a chance at the NFL, that is the money you want to go after. That money is solid, liquid, and the benefits are much more than NIL money. If your situation is that you only want to play college ball, then go for the money, but remember the money after your 4-5 years is much greater, so you need to make sure whatever your post football plan is not sabotaged by the 4-5 years of NIL. Because you won't see all of that money more than likely.

NIL is a good thing, but don't let it be THE thing.

PART 4 >>> UNDERSTANDING THE GAME

Perfect Your Craft

This sport is your art. Everything you do, every play you make, route you run, block you make- it's all part of your craft. So, take pride in that.

My church has a saying that inspires me.

It goes, "Excellence honors God and inspires people."

Make your work excellent. Perfect your craft. Inspire people and bring honor to your God, your name, your loved ones, etc.

This is your life. You only have one chance at this, so work hard and improve your skills. The better your skills are, the easier this recruiting process is. We have talked a lot about the politics around this business, but the reality is that your main priority should be your game.

When those Friday night lights come on, the spotlights are on, and its show time. It is your time to show college coaches what they need to see. That you can help their program win games.

Whatever that takes.

The Relentless Pursuit

Tom Brady posted a video on his Instagram before the 2021 Superbowl with the following dialogue:

"In this journey, there is no final destination. There is only the next one. In the pursuit of perfection, the only thing that counts is the journey itself. The pursuit itself. And those who give their lives to it, this moment and the focus required to seize it, this fight and the commitment required to face it. Because there's no such thing as perfect. There is only the relentless pursuit of perfection. That is our cause. That is what makes us a team. And that is why we're still here. So, once more into the fray. To live and die on this day."

This quote is important with football. There is never an end destination, just "the next one."

The next play, the next game, the next season, the next championship, the next school. You win a championship, that's great, but go win *the next one.*

You lost a state title, that sucks, but go win *the next one.*

Whatever your journey is, you must never stop chasing perfection. Push and keep pushing.

The relentless pursuit of perfection is what will get you the best opportunity to achieve your wildest dreams.

Thank You!

Thank you, guys, for checking out the book. I will continue to push content and useful information your way as a gift of my appreciation. Please don't hesitate to reach out. I will do my best to get back with you.

By the way, all this advice will carry over to your life after football. Networking, learning, and chasing greatness applies in every field of work.

Most Importantly

With everything in me, I pray that you chase your dream. You have one shot at life. If this is important to you, do everything you can to make it happen. I'm rooting for you. I pray that my mistakes can help at least one person achieve their dreams. That's why I coach.

This is my purpose. Find yours!

Comment on the chapters if you have questions or email me at macefarq@gmail.com

Please remember to **SHARE** if you find this useful! Appreciate you guys.

Coach Mace

COACH
MASON FARQUHAR

MASON FARQUHAR HOLDS A MASTER'S DEGREE IN SPORTS LEADERSHIP FROM THE UNIVERSITY OF TULSA AND A BACHELOR'S DEGREE IN ORGANIZATION AND MOTIVATION FROM THE UNIVERSITY OF OKLAHOMA. WITH A ROBUST BACKGROUND IN COACHING, MASON HAS DEDICATED EIGHT YEARS TO DEVELOPING ATHLETES AND TEAMS, INCLUDING FIVE YEARS AT THE COLLEGIATE LEVEL AND THREE YEARS WITHIN HIGH SCHOOL PROGRAMS.

HE IS DETERMINED TO USE HIS EXPERIENCE TO INSPIRE PEAK PERFORMANCE IN HIS PLAYERS.

D1 BOUND
THE ULTIMATE GUIDE
TO COLLEGE FOOTBALL RECRUITING

Made in the USA
Las Vegas, NV
14 December 2024

14124340R00056